MESSAGES FROM
ABOVE:
YOUR MAGAZINE FOR LIFE

GINO MASSARO

Paperback: 978-1-961438-50-7
eBook: 978-1-961438-51-4
Library of Congress Control Number: 2023914043

Ordering Information:

Prime Seven Media
518 Landmann St.
Tomah City, WI 54660

Printed in the United States of America

TABLE OF CONTENTS

CHAPTER 1

HEAVEN AND THE WORD

Words have unsuspected force. They are a storm or a gentle wind. They are the pelting downpour or a storm that waters the farmland.

Knowledge is nothing by itself. What you know, must become a part of your life.

In that way, encounters take place that give things a different color.

But who still enters into a dialogue with himself? Who dares to voice the questions everyone asks in their heart?

A star is like a human life: it disappears between myriads of others. And yet each star, each human being, is a universe. When he dies, everything dies and yet everything lives on.

Why a heaven? Why a human being? Why my-self? Why life and death, the tormentors and the victims, why good and evil?

And what is behind that? Chance, fate, a just God or simply the Unknown who rises far above our questioning? WHY?

Because the same heaven arches above us. Because we are of the same workmanship. Because we are all human beings. And because the word – if it is sincere – can be a help, the outstretched hand of a friend.

CHAPTER 2

THE SOURCE THAT EACH OF US HAS DEEP WITHIN

Who am I that all of this happens to me? That need is the core of our self. Our burning fire in the hearth. Something mysterious. Something that makes us what we are. But who allows weakness to force its way in? The one can save us, the other threatens us with destruction. Why those differences between one human and another? Where does the one get his strength from and how does the other come by his tendency to be dejected and to give up the fight?

For each man and each woman can find that strength inside themselves. There is a source of strength in us, with an energy a thousand times greater than that of the sun. But who still knows how to find that source? It is hidden under the weeds, becomes overgrown by them. We have no ear for its bubbling.

Every now and then a few deeds are inspired by it and then we forget where it is and sometimes even let it run dry.

For there can be no dividing line between the I and the other. Who believes that he is the center everything revolves around, who refuses to see that he is a part of the community, will one day experience sorrow and bitter poverty. A human being is nothing, when his heart is empty.

You must not let smooth talk, outward appearance or the ranks and positions people hide behind, pull the wool over your eyes. The true human being is someone's inner self. That is where his true wealth lies. That is where his true strength is hidden.

To be in harmony with others, you must first be in harmony with yourself. Then the source that is the origin of our being, of our personality, should be able to flow freely and happily. You have to acknowledge you own needs, to let your most inner self blossom instead of pushing it away, as happens all too often. You need to know how to find the way to yourself, to the source that wells up in every human heart. At the same time, that is the first step towards the others. For all too often you feel that you are an ordinary person, just like everybody else. That is why you must first bring to life this 'other' deep within, your one true self.

You must discover your source, find out the meaning of the current that carries us along. Everyone must grow towards his destiny. You have to discover and accept yourself as you are.

When you clearly show others the self that slumbers deep inside everyone, only then do you get the face of a human being. The unconscious, bitter hatred ebbs away. A human opens up to himself. Resentment and regret fall away and with them his hatred disappears. He can muster the strength to accept the world and other people as they are. Human beings are only human, after all.

We all know that we carry a voice deep within, that talks to us in a clear and simple language, a voice we all too often smother. Because it is demanding and uncompromising. A human being does not submit to what is unacceptable. A human being treats the treasure within him, his humanity, with the necessary respect. He refuses to let it be trampled on. No matter what price he must pay for it.

True wisdom is: to listen to the refusal in your inner self, to respect the human being within, it takes courage to keep harmonizing your life with the demands of the voice inside us that is our truest being.

I know that there is a beast in every human and that life is one great struggle to prevent being dominated by it. And every human runs this risk. For everyone carries this brute violence inside. It lies in wait and we can lose the struggle at any time. We keep our face, our outward appearance, but the human being within us can become a slave and the darkness can destroy us. From the heart of the jungle within us a dark monster leaps out.

It conquers the source within us and gorges on it. Wafer-thin are the screens behind which most people hide their demons.

The inhumanity, the unknown beast within us, can gain control of us. For in each one of us lives the history of humanity, a thousand times a thousand years old. A long chronicle of cruelty, lack of restraint and brutality. Every time a human is born, he inherits the entire past of humanity. If he pays no attention to it, he might collapse under its weight.

The years of childhood are like running water, that floods the field of blossoming humanity. But it can also turn the field into drowned land. This original water needs to last a person's entire life. With this, he slakes his thirst or poisons himself. It is important to watch over a child carefully, while it is still young. At that point, there is nothing more important for a human than starting to live a different life.

For that matter, a child does not first and foremost need all sorts of things. It longs for the others. A child needs to feel every moment the sheltering, dedicated and attentive presence of the one who carried it, of those who wanted it. To give a child something must be: to give yourself. At every opportunity. Then it can shoot up straight and grow deep, strong roots.

The parents sow the child and they also are the earth in which it buds and grows. To the child, they are the entire world. They make clear how things work out there, what should and should not be done. What they do, what they say and who they are leaves its mark on the child. Even if it does not know this yet. For the child will always remain a part of the adult the child will become one day.

What you give a child, it will give back one day. What you refuse a child, it will refuse later. The harm you do to a child, it can inflict later. But if you let the sails of its young ship bulge with the breeze of strength, courage and sincerity, it will keep to a straight course and be able to weather the storms.

The lessons a child really listens to and that shape his personality, are the actions of the adults. To raise a child is to be a living example for your child.

To protect a living creature, whether it is a child or an adult, never means you should reason away the risks of human existence. For life does include a share of suffering. To protect someone means first of all: to teach him to pay attention, to show him the danger around him and most of all within himself. It is: to teach someone to face and overcome the danger.

A child and an adult want to have a trial of strengths. To become what they want to become and what is their calling, they must engage with people through things. Fear and pain are good teachers. Experience makes wise and allows a human being to discover himself.

We must get to know the body, this part of nature within us, and tame it.

A human being must be one whole. He is instinct and common sense. He needs to accept that he is body and spirit. A tree consists of bark and wood. If you peel off the bark, the tree wastes away. If the wood dries out, the bark will rot and the tree will die. Who wants to be only core wood and refuses to know anything about the past, is not really a human.

A human being must accept his mistakes, he must be able to acknowledge his weak points. As soon as he acknowledges them, he has already half conquered them. For a human being the past should, first of all, mean a measure of experience from which he learnt wise lessons.

A person's past can be a lot like weeds in a garden or a climbing plant on a wall. Budding plants are smothered by it, the heaviest stones dislodged. Yes, the past can hurt a person. Not that you can deny or erase the past. You always carry it with you, it is engraved in your inner self. It is your personal piece of history, a chunk of history like no other. But you have to break free from it. Then, building on that experience, you can move on without forgetting or betraying the past. For life is a journey towards the future. And you must have faith in what is coming.

There is always a chance that someone is better than he seems. We need to find back the way within a human that leads to his deepest source. And we should help him to let it flow once more. Then, the resurrection of a human being takes place. THE REAL ONE. For a human being may be tied to the past, he is also tied to the future.

In nearly every person something unchanging lies hidden, surrounded by a thick shell. To find it, you in any case have to believe it exists.

When someone once has reached self-realization, when he has connected with the source within him, who can then predict how high he will rise?

There is more to a human being.

Trials are the very means for a human to get to know and rise above himself. Suffering, setbacks and unjust treatment in the heart of the true human being. Only the one who is empty inside, will collapse under them.

Growth never means that a human should forget the past. He must acknowledge it to free himself of it this way. Then he will gain a better understanding of himself and his final goal.

CHAPTER 3

A HUMAN BEING ALONE: A STONE

Human being who ignore each other, are just like stones in a pile. And a human being alone is a stone a in a field, hard and unable to produce anything.

A human being can be lonely surrounded by other people. But who is open to the world, who is ready to lend a helping hand, who feels solidarity with all others, will never be lonely, even if he were to live like a hermit. If you reach out with your hands, others will grasp them. A human being is never lonely because he is alone. He can always find someone else to go through life with.

Withdrawing into yourself, keeping other out and ruthless egoism, are as many deadly poisons. They make a person afraid. They isolate.

A human being's look is enough to break open someone's loneliness. And one day, that look will come. But you need to believe it exists first.

A human being is never lonely, as long as he knows he is a tiny, yet indispensible part of a whole, of a mighty and countless mass, of humanity. A human being is never lonely, as long as he does not see his own self as the focal point of his life. A human being is never lonely and even never weak, when he lets his energy join the boundless ocean of all human energy.

A human being can only escape unhappiness and loneliness, if he knows that there is someone else even lonelier and unhappier than he, someone who is waiting for a hand to reach out to him.

Condemning others means: to lock yourself up inside yourself, to condemn yourself to being alone. For the other is not first of all an enemy, but rather a potential ally. And even those who fight against you, can still help you. For everyone can learn from their enemies.

You must have faith in humanity.

In order to get someone else to understand you, to make him come to you, to end your loneliness, you have to be sincere. Then, a dialogue will grow. And the dialogue between one human being and another: that is life.

Who jumps to the conclusion that all other are hostile to him, is a lonely person. You must share other people's sorrow, then they will let you share in their joy as well. And in that way, you will never feel lonely.

Helping others is the best way of all to help yourself.

Sometimes a word or even a look is enough to prevent something irreversible, or on the hand, to trigger it. We must pay attention to people around us. To their silent cry for help.

Always remember that someone else may not be able to do without you, because you can break open the loneliness that is choking him.

Who gives, receives.

Loneliness fathers violence and despair.

Who is stimulated by an ideal, who strives for a great, common ideal, is not lonely. The violence of a lonely person is aimed first of all against himself.

Joining a large crowd does not mean you will stop feeling lonely. You will remain alone, as long as you do not take part in a great, common enterprise.

First, you must overcome the loneliness inside yourself. In order to meet each other, to break open each other's loneliness, two beings must have the same expectations for the future. Human beings are not alone in this world. They are no more than a part of nature. If they destroy it, they will at some point be as lonely as if they were in the middle of the wilderness. If a human being feels alone, if he is anxious and afraid, then that is because he severed his ties with nature. A human being and nature form one living whole, but it is a combination that can perish.

If they are separated from each other, both the one and the other become an infertile chunk of stone. And if human beings do not appreciate nature or even destroy it, they deny and destroy themselves. When every stranger can be an enemy, a human being lives in fear and loneliness. A human being is never more lonely than right in the middle of a crowd.

There is no loneliness worse than other people's indifference. And everyone can, at some point, become the victim of that indifference and suffer because of it. Why, then, do we not reach out to those who are lonely? No one can tell in advance whether he will not also stand alone one day. Loneliness is a mirror. You can see yourself in it as you were and are.

Loneliness is also a test. Who did not let the source within himself dry up, can manage to pull through. Loneliness shows a human being as he really is. Who knows things is often lonely. But then that loneliness is the price you have to pay for your knowledge. Then you have to accept that with determination and with your head held high.

Sometimes you must choose loneliness, if it is the only way to remain loyal to yourself and others.

Love can transform the stony soil into fertile earth from which life shoots up.

CHAPTER 4

LOVE

If you love someone, the other is a world by him or herself. You are never finished with your journey of exploration in this world. The other is the water that quenches your thirst and at the same time the thirst that makes you want to drink.

Everyone of us is yearning for love. And you must trust that it will come. For thoughts open up a channel.

Love means: to make each other feel safe.

For a life without love has absolutely no value.

Sometimes you stop loving and choose for so-called common sense. But then you forget that our whole life is an act of love and one day you will discover that the game is up.

There is nothing to be gained in life unless you have love.

Love never has anything to do with compulsion.
Love is joy, freedom and strength.
Love is the very thing that kills the fear of life.

Where love is missing, fear and boredom lie in wait.

Love is based on the law of attraction. If you feel the need for love, you must let it guide you. As long as you do not lose sight of the fact that love is life itself, you will meet with it some day.

There is at least one other person with the same desire.
There is at least one other person for whom you are the only one he or she is looking for, for whom you are irreplaceable. And he or she exists exclusively for you. Only, there are too many people who are afraid to love someone.

Love is speed. Love is full of enthusiasm. Love is: daring to take risks. Who is economical with his feelings, does not really love another and is not loved either. Love is freehanded. Love is extravagantly generous. But love is also an interaction. Who gives much, will ultimately receive much as well. For only what we give, is our inalienable property.

Well then, if you want to gain something with regard to love, you first need to get down from your pedestal, become enthusiastic, be ready to give yourself completely.

In order to accomplish the physical union, each one needs to give up his or her bad habits, to take a step towards the other, to think only of the other person. Then only will you find the other who will find you in turn, but you also find yourself.

To love someone does not mean: to lock up the other.

Instead, true love wants the other to blossom, wants him or her to grow in a natural way. To love means that you do not maim or dominate the other, but rather stand by his side, help him along on his path. Love is diametrically opposed to lust for power.

You must accept the other as he is. Find pleasure in what makes him happy. Love him as he is, without imposing restrictions. Accept his beautiful and ugly sides, his faults and good traits. Those are the conditions of love and of a good relationship. For love includes the virtues of tolerance, forgiveness and respect for the other.

There is no foolproof way of living together. There are numerous paths leading to happiness and inner peace. Everyone can find his own path, if he makes an effort to understand the other. And to understand the other, you have to imagine yourself in his or her situation. You have to step outside yourself, to look beyond your own fantasies. You have to see reality as it is.

It shows wisdom if you can recognize and admit that someone else does not love you anymore. And that life goes on in spite of that cruel discovery. A wise person recognizes that love is an interaction. If the other person does not open up to you, it is better for you to be reserved as well. Otherwise you suffer twice. And in vain, for the suffering of the one who loves, does not awaken love. At most, the other will feel sorry for you, but feeling sorry for someone is the opposite of love.

There is only one path for each couple. For each couple is one of a kind. Each being is one of a kind by itself and from the meeting of two beings, something truly unique emerges. Everyone can find the other with whom he wants to build or rebuild his life. Everyone must invent his own way of loving. There is no example for that. Everyone is king. Everyone must begin at the beginning.

A human being is not just a body. Love is not just a meeting of two bodies. Love is the sharing of words and looks, of hope and fear. Who prunes love does not even know it. It consists of physical pleasure and shared expectations. Those two are inextricably linked, just like the branches of a tree cannot exist without its roots.

What is a tree without fruit? What is love without a purpose, without a future? A child is the natural future of every married couple. The face of their child is their own face. Sometimes a tree cannot bear fruit. But then another purpose is needed. Then, you need to build another future together. For the future that you build together is the foundation that keeps a couple together and gives them life.

Life is one whole. There is happiness and unhappiness, birth and death. To want the one without the other is to say 'no' to life. To be willing only to see the one or the other means you condemn yourself to going through life blinkered. Then, you maim life itself.

None of us can do without the knowledge that there is a future. Everyone of us feels a need to leave a trace of his or her passage through humanity. And a child is the trace a man and a woman can leave behind together.

The river that flows to sea can follow all kinds of courses. It is of vital importance that it flows to sea and does not flow away somewhere in the sand. A married couple must be open to others, otherwise their marriage will not succeed. A human couple has to create children or artworks or happiness for those around them. They have to pass on their love. For the love that locks itself up, will wither and die like a plant without light. Children, artistic creations, other people, the world, are the sun and the water that allow love to live.

When you divorce, end your marriage, you cut deep into life. You must be quite sure that what you gain by that outweighs the grief you will feel. When you cut too many branches off a tree, sometimes it dies. And besides, you have to consider the other person, all other people. Consider everyone who feels safe under those branches.

Love is: to succeed in giving someone else self-confidence.

The harmony between two people, their happiness, is partly a result of their willingness to build up that harmony and that happiness together. Love is not just a miracle born from a single encounter. Love is what you make of it day by day. You must intend to make something of it.

CHAPTER 5

DEATH

Death does not leave us.
Why does death exist anyway?

Sooner or later that ordeal is there in all its insufferable cruelty. And yet, no matter how unacceptable, you must learn to accept death.

You must not forget that death exists. You must not forget that it strikes around us, that it can take our dearest possession. And we should not think that we are safe from its violence. We must not lose sight of that. We have to remember that grief will also strike us and that the wound will never heal. And yet life will have to go on.

Why does death exist? Why must we live with it?
An afterlife?
A good, righteous God who takes the souls unto him?
Why does life exist? Why does death exist?

There always is something unfair to us about the death of someone you love or the death of a child.

A tree is uprooted, while you had such much wanted to live in its shade.

A tree is cut down, even before it has born fruit.

The cycle of death is only broken by activities. For action is life.

You must be willing to put death in checkmate. With deliberate action, you must deny despair a chance. The death of people you love is like a whirlwind that wants to suck us in. You can let yourself go, let yourself be swept away. But it is better to avoid the whirlwind. You need to believe in yourself and to have the will to keep on living.

Having faith is: wanting to live. To want the fullness of life in spite of death.

Having faith is: believing in life.

You fight death by moving on in life.

For life drives death away.

Every spring the trees bud again. Autumn and winter are nothing more than seasons of the year, just like spring and summer. Human beings must learn to see death as a part of life.

You should not want to force the natural order of things.

There is a time for grief and another time to overcome it.

Remaining loyal to those who died does not mean that you should lock yourself up in your grief. You must keep plowing your furrow through life: deep and absolutely straight. Just as they would have done themselves. Or as you would have done with them. Or for them. Remaining loyal to the ones who died means living as they would have lived. And keeping them alive inside yourself.

It means passing on their attitude, their words, their message to other people.
To a son, a brother or to strangers. Just to others, no matter who. Then, the pruned life of those who passed away, will bud again and again.

Only from your own inner self and from your own strength can you summon the will to give the final blow to death and desperation. But after that, you must focus on other people. On life with its manifold aspects. A tree remains standing where it stands first of all because of its roots. But without any sun it will die.
Others are our sun.

A human being will die one day. Some day his life will end. Those you love, die. But always children will be born. There will always be people. Life with its billions of faces goes on, reproduces. And the others, the people a deceased leaves behind and those who are born, let the dead live on. Death can only be destroyed by our solidarity with others.

Death always is the crucial test.
An emptiness suddenly gaping at us.
There is no point in walking away. You must learn to look at it. And then find a way to overcome it.

People nowadays, our modern society, do not want to have anything to do with death and misery. They prefer to camouflage those things. But then they do strike us like meteorites hurtling down towards us from space.

No one escapes.

They are simply a part of our life.

Each human being must learn to face them.

Everything that threatens life must be banished. You must defend life against death. Of course you have to sacrifice life sometimes. But that is to protect humanity from the guerrillas of death: the political systems that use death as a tool of power and their henchmen. But an idea is only great, a cause is only just, when the protection of all life is central to it.

Against the fear of death there is only one remedy: you must live and open up to the beauty of the world. You must become one with the mystery of heaven with its starry splendour. You must consciously become part of the great whole, the universe full of life, that is constantly moving.

You need to face death, because it is unavoidable anyway. But you must not be afraid of it, not admit defeat in advance. You must accept its existence and join battle with it. And be able to muster the necessary wisdom, when our time will come.

When death strikes around us, the people it hits, will live on in the memory of those who are left behind. They live on, because the universe is a eternal whole that unfolds in ever-changing forms.

Human beings are a small part of that universe and thereby of eternity. Just as those of the universe, their forms change. Their death, the moment life falls apart, is just a passage. For life in the cosmos never stops, it is eternal. And death is just the end of one form of life, that will be reborn elsewhere in a thousand other guises.

CHAPTER 6

LIFE

Life is treacherous like the sky, sometimes cloudless, sometimes threatening. Life is generous like the spring rains, wild and cruel like a hurricane. Life destroys and then again provides abundance. That is life and you must love it. You have to know how to recognize its beauty, the brightening during the storm and its majestic grandeur. For: life is humanity and the cosmos.

Life always fluctuates between light and darkness, between hope and despair, between worries and a sense of peace. You can regain your grip on life time and time again. Who believes that he has taken the final hurdle by now, is mistaken. There will always be another hurdle, another battle. Once the battle stops, all that lies before us is a barren plain, without barricades that need to be stormed. Then it is time to die.

To be born in itself means to fight, to have feelings of unrest, to be squeezed out of the safe, warm shelter of your mother's body. But you must accept this battle and these feelings of unrest. For they are life itself.

Life describes an arc, just like the sun. One day it slowly begins to set. You have to prepare for that time. To accept it. You have to be aware that the second half of life is life also. That it can be as rich as the first half. There are small hours of twilight that are more beautiful that the dawn. You simply have to want it. To guide other people and yourself with the peace that reigns within us.

Life is a blueprint, a plan you must make for yourself. He really counts who leaves his mark in the tangible world. He really lives who is active. For life is founding, building, continually building. Stone on stone, idea after idea, one act after another. Life is getting to know yourself, getting to know the world in order to be able to change oneself and others through that knowledge.

In that way, you find peace within. The only peace that is lasting.
In that way, you make people's lives less cruel and you can offer a look, a kind word and a helping hand to those who ask for it.

You have to make plans that allow you to grow spiritually. Make plans that lift up life. Plans that make us strive for the heights instead of the muddy ditches. Plans with style that make life stylish. And that give a human life the chance to unfold, to reach a higher plane.

You do not build anything by rebelling against something or someone. If you want to enjoy the fullness of life, it must not be directed against, but aimed at something.

Aimed at something!

Life is one and indivisible, one single plant. And who lashes out at others to hit the outside world, also hits himself.

Life is a tree that is bent this way and that by the storm. You must hold on tight to the branches, you must be willing to cling to them, until the wind, the storm, dies down. At least, if it ever dies down.

In life, nothing is sorted once and for all.

You always have to stay on guard. Braced for an unexpected gust of wind. You have to be able to capture the beauty of an evening, of a morning, of a single second. For the day after that, yes, the very next second can be swept by storms.

You must not let yourself go. You must not let yourself be overwhelmed by grief. You must join battle with it and not keep it alive by watering it with tears together. Someone who has sorrow and feels afraid, does not need another cry of misery, but a voice sounding more powerful than his own that gives him courage. Putting out a fire is not the same thing as allowing it to keep on raging or letting burn you in complete submission.

First, you have to banish the fear from someone's thoughts. To calm him down. To keep repeating that there are always opportunities you can seize. All the happiness you can wish for, is possible as long as there is life.

Life does not just mean to let yourself be carried along by the stream. For one day it may just happen that you do not stay afloat anymore. At some point a whirpool can suck us to the bottom or into the quicksand.

Life is: knowing that you are alive.

Life is: wanting to live.

Life is: believing in life.

A thought can be a seed that brings either death or life when it germinates. But it should be a germ of life. You must force yourself to banish all those sombre thoughts that shroud our mind in a persistent mist. Thoughts must lean towards life, form a source of life. And if someone cannot do this, if someone does not have the strength for this at some point, he must dismiss all thoughts, to stop thinking altogether, to let himself be overwhelmed by sounds and impressions, by staying active and listening to other people's talk. You need to know how give life hand. And sometimes you need to summon the courage to simply run away.

Thoughts cannot be poison. Life cannot not be denied either in words, or in thoughts.

Life is: sharing together. Not to stay locked up inside yourself.

Life is: being open to the world.

You can never believe in yourself too much. People still know their own life force far too little.

Life is: to dare to pull down the walls you have built up around yourself.

Life is: to overcome the restrictions you have imposed on yourself. Life is: to come out on top again and again.

A person's mind, will, thoughts can multiply the forces of life. But to be able to do that, you first have to want it. It is the willpower, the inner world of thoughts, those invisible powers, that allow us to grasp life as with outstretched, expectant hands.

Our thoughts can master those walls and restrictions. Respecting those thoughts and putting them into practice: that is the great adventure of life.

In life there is a straight path that you can follow, for no matter what reason.

It is the acts that make a person's life and judge it. Not the words. Nor the intentions. A single word, a single thought can get an act started or stop it. That is why we must be careful with our thoughts and words. They are cancerous growths or sources of energy. They tear apart or bring together. A word, a thought can be an act in themselves.

The ordeal is the moment of truth. Before that time, you never fully know someone. Then suddenly the storm comes. Trees are blown down. Some you thought were not planted all that firmly, bend down but straighten up again; others you thought were strong, break off. The ordeal is merciless. You get to know someone. Who is a zero, collapses even if he looks as if he were made of marble. There always is an ordeal of some kind in someone's life.

You need to focus your life not on the past, but on the future. For life is after all a river flowing to tomorrow. Nothing can reverse its course. That is why the day of tomorrow is more important than that of yesterday. Clinging to the past is the same thing as becoming entangled in masses of dead, rotting winter plants that slow down the current, that smother the joy of living. Then you will drown.

You have to keep swimming in the middle of the current. And remember that the present has its sources in the past and flows into the future. You have to know how to adapt to the course of things. Yesterday is finished. Our roots lie in the past, but the fruits on the tree ripen today and will be harvested tomorrow.

To take a different course, to change, does not have to mean that you deny yourself. You can also rise above yourself.

Everyone of us turns life into an entirely different, very personal experience. And from every experience, whether is enjoyable or bitter, a human being must learn something. There is not a single occurrence in an human life that is without meaning. No day, no setback is useless. At least: if you do not stand motionless, staring at it as if hypnotized, as if you are the prey of a snake. You must use it as a support to push off from.

In each life there will come a moment when an abyss splits open in front of or next to someone, within a person. Life is: managing not to fall in. Life is: daring to look into it and yet remain at a safe distance. Life is progress, it means growing, blossoming in happiness, but also: learning from your unhappiness. Barren times and stormy days we must turn into moments of purification and renewed strength to reach a higher plane, not in comparison with others, but with ourselves. Life is unfolding yourself. Fully realizing what you in fact already are.

Life is knowing what comes first in someone's life. What you value the most. To place things in their order of importance. And that is different for everyone. Everyone must make his own plan. You should not imitate others. Everyone has to find his own path. And to get himself to the point of actually following it. For the life you do not want to live, that you had in you, but that you have smothered, slowly becomes a destructive force. Like a current continually growing stronger, it undermines the personality and destroys all sorts of chances of happiness. The future is strangled by complaints about the life you missed out on.

Living means creating your own world. Finding your own peace. And that is different for everyone. It can even be born from someone's unhappiness, as long as he or she manages to overcome it. Everyone can reach that point. But you do have to want it. First, you must know that peace will only come if you make contact with others. Whether it is family ties or the togetherness of a community, whether it is a contact with words or with thoughts; that does not matter much. As long as there are contacts. You will not feel satisfied if you remain a lone tree. It is the forest that gives the trees meaning and makes them strong.

For life is to stand with both your feet firmly in this world and enjoy it. You live only then, when you want also that joy, when you maintain it. You must not give the gray weeds of dejection a chance. Life is making an effort for all kinds of things. Life is just being yourself. Attracting and repelling. Accepting and rejecting. To live is to create!

CHAPTER 7

THE DEPTHS THAT SWALLOW A HUMAN BEING

Who makes fame and what other people think of him his goal in life, is always panting like a thirsty dog. He never finds peace. For a famous name and the high esteem of others are as changeable as clouds in the sky on a windy day.

Longing for fame, striving for honour, lust for power are lingering diseases, ailments that slowly eat people away and destroy their personality. For you can only let harmony take root in your own being. Through your own efforts. Everything else is vulnerable, uncertain, soon over.

Striving for honour (except striving to become a different, better person) is a plague. One of the great diseases of humanity, one of the depths he can end up in.

Sometimes you are empty inside and afraid of yourself. Sometimes there is a void, as with a tree of which nothing but the bark is left, and the soul is missing. That makes someone chase after fame and the hustle and bustle of praise and publicity. But the void within keeps rumbling and all those things cannot end that. To achieve that anyway, someone in that situation strives for even greater honour, wants even more bustle. But the void within us keeps growing at the same rate. In the same rhythm.

And there will come a time when the void will gain the upper hand. That depends on all kinds of accidental circumstances. It may not begin until you are past fifty or perhaps not until you are old. But then that void will be there, as deep as an abyss. Fame and celebrity could never lessen it; on the contrary, they only made it deeper day in day out.

You can build castles in the air, keep chasing after success and publicity; it remains an attempt to reach the bottom of a bottomless depth. The outside world will get an impression that dances like a light shining on a rippling surface. Against your better judgement, you hope it will stop being a flickering blur, that it will assume a solid form. All of this can result in an even more anxious searching for more of that fame and publicity. Unless you suddenly discover that the search will never end and that what you miss, will always be greater than what you possess. You have hollowed yourself out. That can break someone.

Achieving something, what does that really mean?

It is a flight that masquerades as earning huge amounts of money.

But that is not the same thing as succeeding in life.

Living, wanting to make something of your life, can never mean reducing it to just wanting to possess things, products, money. Making something of your life cannot mean merely piling up soulless material. Living in such a way really is the same thing as slowly sinking under the weight of the things around us.

Was that living? Then what an abyss that was! And what did you really live for, then? The void in our life can become too deep. Our life goes by with grasping for all kinds of things that melt like ice between our fingers. We toil and slave to hold just a handful of water. We discover that possessions are just a fleeting pleasure and we continually have to have more. When we become aware of that, we often totter on the edge of a depression. That is the illness of a life without a purpose that makes life worth the pain and the trouble. Such a breakdown is a protest of our innermost being against wasting our life, against maiming and lowering it.

A life limited exclusively to your own self is no life. It is a path that only leads to the abyss of loneliness, to the sinking feeling of being a failure.

If we pay attention to ourselves only, if we give in to the laws of a time in which you first of all have to stand up for yourself, we soon imagine that we are working to our own advantage. It seems that we are piling up things. But in fact, we are throwing them into the abyss. Only the human being who opens up to another person, makes his life truly rich. For the richness of a human life consists in enthusiasm and a happy mood. And that only emerges when you have renounced yourself. Who only wants to have and keep something for himself, lives in a desert. He will be buried under his own possessions. Who takes a step towards others, lives with others, walks around in an oasis.

The city, the far too big cities, are like diseased growths, like enormous tumors. There, people become uprooted and ignore each other. And the cities keep getting bigger. They are depths that become deeper and deeper and where brotherly habits are lost. The quiet glance and the smile disappear there. In those cities people tumble around like grains of sand, they mean nothing there. There, we must bring back peace and joy, bring people closer together again by opening their eyes and their hearts for each other.

Violence is the evil of a city that is far too big. For violence is a wild rebellion unexpectedly breaking out against the empty, pointless life someone leads. Violent people, who are at loggerheads with others, at odds with themselves, destruction and self-destruction. Violence picks someone as its victim, as a target, sometimes because of the colour of his skin and sometimes for no reason. Aggression is the drug of this age.

Violence is a random eruption of energy, a destructive stream that we must restrain with dykes and dams.

Our hard, unrelenting society tosses the weaker people on the garbage heap. It is our unwritten laws that crown money and achievements king. It already is an established habit to glorify violence and recommend the flight from reality into the dreamworld of drugs and alcohol. Everywhere inequality that makes the rich and the strong even richer and stronger and the poor and the weak even poorer and weaker. Our society still too often resembles a jungle, a concentration camp where no fellowship exist anymore and everyone goes his own way without caring about other people at all. All of this leads to those lost lives, lives that have already been given up, trapped as they are in dead-end alleys.

Were human beings made for such a life? I could not live without the hope that there will come a different time some day. Then, life will be different. Then, human beings will be able to take off the chains of inequality; then they will be able to get rid of the weight of a society that crushes them. A different time: people without unnecessary burdens. People who can finally deal with their problems for a change, can engage with truly important questions and underlying, more finely nuanced emotions, such as happiness, the how and why of their life, the dialogue about death. But a human being who is hungry, a human being who is afraid, cannot think about that at leisure. He is groping blindly.

Yes, we are still living in a pond.

Yes, human beings still live a prehistoric age.

And that is exactly what we need to get out of

For there are billions of people who suffer hunger and their number keeps growing. Right now, there are already more than seven billion people on this planet. Tomorrow - within the next fifty years - there will be more than nine billion people. The inequality between people, the abundance of some and the want of most will then no longer be an insult to human dignity only. No matter what the colour of your skin may be, this inequality will be a threat to us all. For we are standing with our back to the abyss. Not wanting to see it, does not mean that it is not there anymore. To ensure that we do not keeping balancing on the edge, we first must dare to look at it. Then, we must find a way to get away from there.

Justice and equality must become enduring values. Not just because of moral considerations, but by now also because honesty and equal opportunities for everyone are the least dangerous paths. But to get humanity enthusiastic about those new paths, it is not enough for a few people to choose them. All people and first of all those who do not suffer hunger themselves anymore, must show understanding for this. For the thoughts and will of a human being form an immeasurable force.

The idiot is not the one who says there is a problem, but that it is not yet time to do something about it. The idiot is the one who closes his eyes, buries his head in the sand and refuses to listen. For one day the problem will come knocking on his door, the disease will infect him and there will be no making up for lost time.

Humanity stands at a crossroads. For the first time, a future lies open before us the looks of which we can predict. Every year tens of millions more people, billions of people, and an industry that destroys the soil, the water and even the air. And at the end of that road violence, disorder and hunger await.

But there is also another path. That of the will to turn around. The will to use the power of human beings to their salvation and not to their unhappiness. And only one source of power can accomplish this: that of the human conscience. Each person who feels involved, must choose this other path, spurred on by his conscience. For it leads to a peaceful building up of the world. When a human being wants to, he can fill up the depths along his path. Next to a dead tree he can always plant a strong and healthy tree. But he does have to want it. He must dare to see the risks and warn about them. He must not give in to thoughtless convenience . Then there will be a green future and the climate will be mild again.

CHAPTER 8

DESTINY

Is fate something real? Are we held in the palm of a hand that randomly saves or crushes us? And is that force something that belongs to us? Does it live outside us? Has it plotted a course we must follow from our cradle? Should we believe in destiny?

Is that how our lives are guided? Are we free in our choices or are we driven to our destiny like blind people powerless to resist?

What is fate actually? It is a name a human being gives to events. A chain he creates in his mind to connect separate facts. A chain that turns him into a prisoner, if he submits to it. But also a chain he will always want to break. Even though it is heavy and appears to offer so much resistance, breaking it is the deepest meaning of a human life.

A human being is always facing two paths. He must choose between them. Two paths present themselves to his vision, two destinies. And with every step, there is a new crossroads. Again, two paths; again, two destinies. And on it goes until the last second of his life.

Nothing has been decided in advance. There never is just one path or a single destiny. Remember that you can and even must make a choice. But you do have to want to choose. And to believe that that is possible. You make your own destiny. And there is always a way out. As long as there is just a glimpse of life, there is still hope that you can make a choice, that you can still change either yourself or the world.

A human being is not just an assembly of cogwheels, a little pile of material. He is first of all a being that can take decisions and everyone who knows what he wants, has it in him to make something new of his life, with his cogwheels and with his physicality. For each human being is one of a kind. And each human being should want to be that, even when he feels solidarity with everyone.

Fate.

Each moment of life the cards are dealt again. Yesterday we were ill, today we once more glow with health. Today happiness and peace reign, tomorrow misery and despair. But we can always build up something new with what happens to us. As long as a human being is alive, he can always build up something new, even if ruins are all he has got.

For a human being is one whole. Thoughts are vague and willpower wavering, if too much is demanded of the body. The realm of thought is like a jar of water. It can become murky or be muddied, when the jar itself gets dirty or full of mud.

To prevent life slipping through his fingers without him even noticing it, a human being must control his desires, sometimes even restrain them. He has to be aware that health is a capital possession that he cannot use wastefully. For it is that capital possession that makes him rich. If he wants to maintain it, he must know where to draw the line and how to live modestly.

Some sources of pleasure are attractive and quick, but they are a slippery slope on which you have to brace yourself. Such pleasures are often very tangible, but in the end of minor importance. That is why a human being must be able to say 'no' to them. If he gets involved with them too often, they can stop him from reaching a durable joy in life on a higher plane. Once more, you have to make a choice. You have to know what is truly important. The exciting, but fleeting warmth of alcohol or the clear, fresh water of life.

A human being can lack a purpose in life that is greater than he. He may already have given up the hope of living a life that is right for him. He may have given up on reaching the top and intend to chug along day in day out without even knowing where he is going. Then he can flee along miserable backroads leading to mediocre enjoyments. And he can get lost there. Endanger his body and in that way weaken his courage in life and the realm of his thoughts and be even less motivated for something greater.

To reach the fullness of his humanity, to be truly human, a human being must create a world he is a central part of. That can be a creation: the painting of an artist or the cabinet of a cabinetmaker, the field of a farmer or a page of a writer's manuscript. It can be a family. For a human being needs to be the cornerstone of a temple he builds and maintains himself.

For a human being cannot get by with cold reasonings only. His common sense is a soil that needs water in order to produce fruits. And that water is love, it is other people, it is the hope, the faith that tomorrow a new beauty will blossom in every human being, starting with himself. It is the certainty that a human being can live in joy and peace with himself and others. One day grief will come unexpectedly. That is unavoidable, for death is always near. But then there is the hope that a human being will use that grief and turn it into something positive. He will draw from it the assurance that he must live a better life, on a higher plane. In this fragile wonder life lies hidden.

The magazine of life.

Life is indestructible. In spite of death. Hope is a powerful gust of wind that must blow away despair. The other is a brother rather than an enemy. In order to survive, you have to arm yourself with love and hope. You must try to gather together the scattered pieces our personality is built of.

You must believe in the noble words: brotherhood, duty and respect for human beings.

You must never look with despair at yourself and the world. The forces within us, the forces that can push us upwards, are incredibly strong. Our willpower is a force of unknown dimensions. We can always rebuild things if we only want to.

You must speak words of love and not of chaos or stormy violence. But you must be willing to risk something to stand up for a certain truth, for a basic principle of togetherness. Sometimes you must be willing to take on the fight with yourself and also with those who allow the demon of inhumanity to get hold of them.

The Royal prerogative of human beings, as well as their heavy burden, is that they must start over again and again, always starting afresh to carry on the torch of hope. Death comes to wash away their footsteps in the sand, like the sea, but in spite of that human beings must start over again and again, master their fears and make a new beginning.

Life begins now and every day. Life is hope!